Camino
to
Santiago

a spiritual companion

To Cynthia on your first (of many)
visits to Santiago.

Compiled by John Rafferty
with photographs by Michael Krier   12/8/2018

redemptorist
p u b l i c a t i o n s

Published by **Redemptorist Publications**
Alphonsus House, Chawton, Hampshire,
GU34 3HQ, UK
Tel. +44 (0)1420 88222, Fax +44 (0)1420 88805
Email rp@rpbooks.co.uk, www.rpbooks.co.uk

A registered charity limited by guarantee
Registered in England 3261721

Copyright © Redemptorist Publications 2016
First published January 2016

Text by John Rafferty
Edited by Mandy Woods
Cover design by Christine Reissland
Internals designed by Eliana Thompson
Photos by Michael Krier
Cover photo: Santiago de Compostela in Spain ©
Manuel ROMARÍS/Moment Open/Getty Images

ISBN 978-0-85231-458-6

A CIP catalogue record for this book is available from the
British Library.

The publisher gratefully acknowledges permission to use
the following copyright material:

Excerpts from *The Jerusalem Bible*, copyright © 1966 by
Darton, Longman & Todd, Ltd and Doubleday, a division
of Random House, Inc. Reprinted by permission.

Poem by Michael Luenig in the story
"Nothing Can be Loved at Speed", © Michael Luenig.

Printed by Portland Print, Kettering, NN16 8UN

Camino Chaplaincy

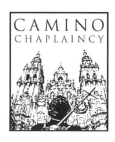

This spiritual companion for pilgrims is being produced under the aegis of the Camino Chaplaincy, which is an apostolate formed of volunteer priests, ministers, religious and lay people. All have walked the Camino to Santiago. The President of the Camino Chaplaincy is Bishop Ralph Heskett C.Ss.R., the Bishop of Hallam, England.

The Camino Chaplaincy aims to provide a ministry of welcome, worship and pastoral support to all pilgrims to Santiago regardless of their denomination or beliefs. The Chaplaincy provides daily services in English in the Cathedral of Santiago and is developing an outreach ministry on the Camino routes. The Chaplaincy very much supports the work of the voluntary pilgrim associations throughout the world, particularly those mentioned in this booklet.

www.caminochaplaincy.blogspot.com

caminochaplaincy@gmail.com

In memoriam

In memory of Hugh Wallace, who died in Santiago de Compostela at the end of his earthly pilgrimage. We also remember all other pilgrims who have died on the Way.

May they rest in peace.

Amen.

For everything there is a season and a time for every purpose under heaven Ecclesiastes 3:1

A time to dream about the Camino and a time to try not to think about it constantly

A time to be unsure and a time to buy the tickets

A time to pack your rucksack and a time to unpack it then pack it again and again

A time to start walking and a time to stop, exhausted

A time to be afraid of new places and people and a time to embrace them

A time to walk with others and a time to walk alone

A time to feel the weight of having packed too much and a time to dump what's unnecessary

A time to feel sore and a time to feel refreshed

A time to feel like giving up and a time to feel inspired by the whole experience

A time to share with others and a time to listen

A time to wonder at the beautiful scenery and a time to do the laundry

A time to enjoy the kindness of local people and a time to decide to learn their language

A time to be irritated by other pilgrims and a time to be tolerant

A time to be angry at the hurts others have caused and a time to forgive them

A time to accept the hurts we have caused and a time to forgive ourselves

A time to realise the journey is coming to an end and a time to prepare to go home

A time to make resolutions for the future and a time to accept that the past cannot be changed

A time to celebrate with new friends and a time to appreciate old friends

A time to arrive and give thanks and a time to plan the next Camino...

John Rafferty

The Pilgrimage to Santiago de Compostela

Each year hundreds of thousands of people walk to Santiago de Compostela in north-west Spain. They take many routes following in the footsteps of pilgrims of the Middle Ages. The most famous route is the Camino Francés, a journey of 778 kilometres from the border of France and Spain to Santiago de Compostela.

This Spiritual Companion

In this booklet thirty-one pilgrims from across the world share their reflections on their pilgrimage to inspire and inform other pilgrims and those interested in the pilgrimage. Their stories may help in preparation for the journey or in accompanying pilgrims on their way.

The Saint

James was a fisherman, son of Zebedee and brother of John.

Legend has it that after preaching the Gospel in Spain, James (Sant Iago) returned to Jerusalem and martyrdom. The site of his tomb in northern Spain was lost for some eight hundred years until a hermit discovered the burial place. The relics were authenticated by the Church and it became a place of pilgrimage which grew into the city of Santiago de Compostela.

In medieval times the pilgrimage grew in popularity. People set off from their homes and walked from all over Europe to Santiago. Religious orders provided shelters along the way in which pilgrims could sleep, and cared for those who were sick or dying.

The Priest and the Paintbrush

Over the last forty years the Santiago pilgrimage has seen a great revival. Perhaps the biggest contribution to this revival came from Father Elías Valiña Sampedro. He was a scholar who, following the historical records, marked out the many routes taken by the medieval pilgrims by painting yellow arrows at approximately every one thousand paces.

The modern pilgrim can follow the yellow arrows from Saint-Jean-Pied-de-Port in France all the way to Santiago on the Camino Francés. Other routes include the Camino Inglés from La Coruña on the north coast, where the English pilgrims arrived by boat, or the 1,000 kilometres from Seville in the south along the Vía de la Plata. These are only a few of the many routes!

The work of Fr Elías and Los Amigos de Santiago also helped build up a huge network of modern refuges for pilgrims just like their medieval counterparts, and all along each route are refuges for rest and sleep (albergues), for a donation or a small charge of a few euros.

Pilgrim Associations

Throughout Spain and in many countries of the world there are now associations which promote the pilgrimage and provide information and support for pilgrims. Information about the English-speaking associations is included in this booklet.

The Compostela

Everywhere pilgrims stop along the way they obtain stamps (sellos) on their Pilgrim Record (also called the Pilgrims' Passport, or Credencial) as evidence of their pilgrimage. When this is presented in Santiago they may be awarded a Compostela – a certificate from the Cathedral.

John Rafferty, Author

John, who also writes under the name
Johnnie Walker, lives in Santiago de
Compostela and regularly walks the Camino
routes. He has published guidebooks to the
Camino Inglés, the Camino Portugués, the
Madrid Route and the Route of Routes in
Santiago. These are available for a donation
from www.csj.org.uk or from his own website:
www.johnniewalker-santiago.blogspot.com.

John has developed the Camino Chaplaincy,
and as a volunteer he coordinates
its activities.

Michael Krier, Photographer

Michael first walked from St Jean to Santiago
in 2003 and returned the following year to
photograph the Camino Francés in order
to gain his Associateship of the Royal
Photographic Society.
He has, subsequently, photographed the
pilgrimage routes from Le Puy, Vézelay
and Tours for the CSJ, as well as the Via
Francigena from Canterbury to Rome. Every
other year he serves as a hospitalero at
Refugio Gaucelmo in Rabanal.

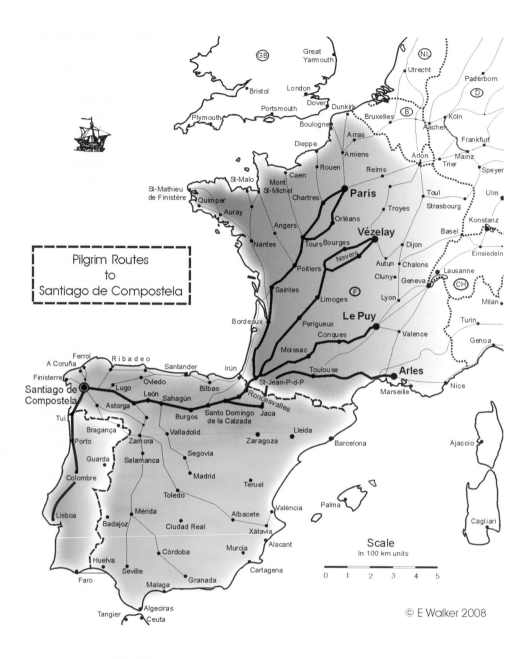

Pilgrim Routes
to
Santiago de Compostela

© E Walker 2008

Scale
In 100 km units

0   1   2   3   4   5

Compiled by
John Rafferty
with photographs
by Michael Krier

In the Beginning – My First Camino

Grant Spangler
United States of America

It was June of 2003, and I dived headlong into Spain.

After several days' sightseeing in Madrid and Barcelona, I'd seen all I'd come to see. I got myself on the Talgo train early the next morning at Sants Estació and we rumbled off towards Pamplona. It should have only taken a few hours, but by 10 a.m. our train had come to a full stop halfway between nowhere and Pamplona. A piece of farm equipment had become firmly ensconced on the tracks up ahead, and we baked in the Spanish sun for several hours. We were eventually hauled back to the coast, changed tracks, and then started over towards Pamplona.

When we finally made landfall in Pamplona it was just after six in the evening. To get to Roncesvalles, there was only one bus per day, and it left at six. When we arrived I was already standing in the coach doorway and was the first off. I made my way through the crowd as quickly as possible, hoping against hope that my bus might still be there. Two young women hefting mammoth packs were engaged in conversation, and obstructing half the platform. I was in a hurry and, feeling somewhat peeved, jumped down onto the tracks and made my way quickly through the train station. The city street revealed a line of taxis but no bus. No bus to Roncesvalles!

I walked back through the station and stood staring at the train. Something told me to pay attention to those two women who had obstructed my path. I waited for them to approach, then spoke to them in Spanish. They replied in Spanish, but with a decidedly American accent. It turns out they were two Spanish teachers from Indiana, the state where I was born. Angela and Linda were on that same train from Barcelona and, like me, were there to walk the Camino de Santiago. I told them of the departure of our "one bus daily", so we made our way into the casco viejo, found a hostel and had dinner.

The next morning we took a taxi up the mountain. Thus began the long journey to Santiago. Linda returned home after a week, but Angela and I walked together the rest of the Way. Thus far I've had eight sojourns to Santiago, but the most profound was this one, the first. Part of it was the embarking into the complete unknown, part of it was the camaraderie of Angela. She referred to herself as "La Ancla", "The Anchor", because she felt she slowed me down. As it turns out, I needed slowing down – my tendency is to walk too far too fast. "Angela" translates as "Angel", and she did indeed seem to be my guardian angel. Her command of the Spanish language had unforeseen benefits. She would engage locals in conversation, enabling me to photograph people being people. A dozen years later and we're still in touch. Things have changed and things have remained the same. The changes on this Camino, however, were profound and permanent.

This is the Camino. Everything you need will be provided. Now go and walk.

[Since I have been longing for many years to visit you,] I plan to do so when I go to Spain. I hope to see you while passing through and to have you assist me on my journey there, after I have enjoyed your company for a while. Romans 15:24

790 Kilometres to Santiago

Silvia Nilsen
South Africa

Its doors are open to the sick and well,

to Catholics as well as to pagans,

Jews, heretics, beggars and the indigent,

and it embraces all like brothers.

La Pretiosa: twelfth-century hymn

Nothing in my sixty years had prepared me for the sight of a hundred pilgrims of all ages and nationalities squashed into a cavernous medieval stone granary, now the pilgrims' hostel at the monastery in Roncesvalles. The smells of sweat and soggy shoes mingled with wintergreen and body odour. Pasted on the wall was a twelfth-century Latin hymn. I thought, "I am the heretic – a Buddhist for over thirty years – but I am being embraced by the Augustinian order that has provided shelter to pilgrims since Sancho de Larrosa, Bishop of Pamplona, built a hospice here in 1127."

Sixty-odd bunk beds were pushed together in twos and it wasn't easy to find a bed next to another female. Luckily there was a bottom bed next to one with a bright pink sleeping bag and a small purple backpack. I guessed they belonged to a woman so claimed the bed next to hers.

The ablutions too were unisex. My tiny camping towel barely covered half of my body and I couldn't decide which half to cover or whether to just cover my face so that any peregrino [male pilgrim] in the shower wouldn't know who the cringing woman was behind the towel.

After dinner, pilgrims walked through the misty rain to the Royal Collegiate Church, where the image of Santa María de Roncesvalles watched over the congregation. My mind wandered during the Spanish service to Mary, mother of Jesus and to the mothers in other religions, Mother Tara, Isis, Devi and Mother Earth – blessed are the mothers. Sant Iago's mother was Salome, sister of Mary. How proud she must be to see her boisterous son so revered, with millions on pilgrimage to his tomb in the cathedral city named after him in Santiago de Compostela.

At the end of Mass held every evening the pilgrims' blessing concludes:

"May our Lady of Roncesvalles grant you her motherly protection; defend you against all dangers of soul and body. Through her intercession may you arrive safely at the end of your pilgrimage, and may almighty God bless you in the name of the Father, Son and Holy Spirit. Amen."

The time had come.

From the Royal Collegiate Church of Our Lady of Roncesvalles

The Rhythm of the Camino

Basil Fallon
Ireland

After six days I feel that I am connecting to the rhythm of the Camino.

The months of preparation are nearly forgotten; making travel arrangements, keeping to exercise plans, checking packing lists, disengaging from work, reassuring people that everything will survive without me, promising to return.

The doubts grew to panic as I did my final packing. Am I fit enough? Should I take another pair of boots, just in case? Now more urgent matters concern me: Where will I sleep tonight? How will I get there?

Starting to walk brings the first hints of the Camino's rhythm. For some it is the "crunch, crunch" of their footsteps on the gravel tracks. For me it is the "click, click" of my walking poles – like a metronome they provide a constant backing track to my journey. They provide a meter for my thoughts. In the morning short and snappy. In the heat of the day slower and more reflective.

The hours spent walking to each day's new destination leave me free from the usual distractions – free to think and pray for friends and loved ones, both dead and alive.

I set and review daily goals: is it 15 kilometres, 20 kilometres or 25 kilometres? I also have time to think about deeper goals, those which could ultimately change my life.

As the metronome is ticking and my thoughts are flowing, I am extremely conscious of my body, and the world around me.

My toes – is that just an ache, or a blister developing? My feet – is that a strain coming on, or just tiredness? Is that a cyclist coming up behind me?

Each day ends with the same routine: the last kilometre is always the hardest; I need to rehydrate; wash myself and my clothes. Only then can I relax and connect with my fellow pilgrims.

Conversations over communal dinners flow easily, despite language barriers. Peregrinos are already in tune with one another.

By now we have all begun to settle into the rhythm of the Camino.

No need to recall the past, no need to think about what was done before. See, I am doing a new deed, even now it comes to light; can you not see it? Yes, I am making a road in the wilderness, paths in the wilds.
Isaiah 43:18–19

The Yellow Arrows

Laurie Dennett
A Canadian living in Spain

Of the many stories about Don Elías Valiña Sampedro – the inventor of "the yellow arrow" and rejuvenator of the Camino in modern times – the following anecdote perhaps captures him best. In Spain it is very well known, though elsewhere, less so.

One day in the Compostellan Holy Year 1982, with fears of terrorism rife in the Basque country, the sight of yellow arrows painted on trees along a track in the Pyrenees aroused the suspicion of the local police – the Guardia Civil. Following the trail, they came upon a battered white van, from which, on seeing them, a small, smiling man emerged. When prompted, he opened the van's back doors to reveal several tins of bright yellow paint and a wet paintbrush.

"Identification!" barked the Guardia.

"I'm Elías Valiña Sampedro, parish priest of O Cebreiro in Galicia."

"And what are you doing with all this?"

"Preparing a great invasion..."

The rest – apart from the Guardia's reply – is history!

The modern-day "invasion" of Spain set in motion in 1982 began as a trickle of pilgrims from other parts of Europe, animated by the first guidebooks to the Camino and by the simple device of the yellow arrows. Long before the new millennium, the trickle had become a broad river, its tributaries the reclaimed historic pilgrimage routes converging on Santiago de Compostela.

The network of associations of "Amigos del Camino" has grown in parallel with the renewal of interest in the pilgrimage to Compostela. With the exception of the French Amis du Chemin de Saint-Jacques, founded in 1951, and the first Spanish group of Amigos, set up in Estella in 1967, they all came into being after 1982. As well as wanting to nurture the pilgrimage, they also wanted to provide facilities for pilgrims.

An example of this is the Confraternity of Saint James, which in 1988 agreed to rebuild and administer a pilgrim albergue (shelter) at a point on the Camino Francés where as yet none existed. Transforming the ruined parish house of Rabanal del Camino into an albergue and running it since then has required a degree of conviction like Don Elías Valiña's faith in "the great invasion"!

If the Lord does not build the house, in vain do its builders labour. Psalm 126:1

Keeping Going

Janet Leitch
Australia

Fighting back tears, I sat on a wall, trying to solve my problem.

It was my first Camino, and my first trip overseas. Nothing was going according to plan. On this road less travelled, the first hotel I stopped at was closed for the August holidays, and the second was closed permanently.

Planning to continue, despite my weariness, I followed the directions but each time I "turned left at the post office" I lost the waymarks. I had spent an hour earlier walking in ever-widening circles searching for a lost waymark.

Sitting on that wall, I couldn't believe what I had done. Here I was in a strange country, with basic language skills, and a return ticket booked for six weeks later. I thought about returning home, but that seemed harder than continuing, which appeared difficult enough. Earlier a man had tried to talk with me, but I didn't know the way of the Camino back then and brushed him aside, nervous of his intentions. I now know that he was trying to help me, as so many do along the way.

Fighting back tears, I looked around and noticed a woman watching me from an upstairs window. To my relief she spoke English and agreed that I could sleep in her home. Her warmth and generosity meant that I had a comfy bed, a hot bath, a delicious dinner, and best of all, I could use her phone to call home. I told her all I knew of the Camino and together we went in search of the lost waymark – which we found at the *old* post office which had relocated across the road some months earlier!

If I could have changed my booking then, I may well have returned home earlier. Fortunately that was not an option, and so instead

20

I continued, one step at a time, taking each day as it came, gladly accepting what the day brought, and learning to trust those I met on a daily basis. My Camino continued, still continues as I walk the many paths, but best of all, it stays with me as I walk life's pilgrimage with its many blessings.

I know how to be poor and I know how to be rich too. I have been through my initiation and now I am ready for anything anywhere: full stomach or empty stomach, poverty or plenty. There is nothing I cannot master with the help of the One who gives me strength.
Philippians 4:12–13

International Fellowship

Jenny Wood
United Kingdom

Without realising it, we had arrived in Estella at fiesta time.

The streets were full of lively families. All the generations were dressed in white and red and excitedly joining in their local celebration. Backpackers were swept along in a red and white tide which ebbed and flowed along narrow streets between the bullring and the town square. In the morning we went round in circles, losing our way completely. Seeing our bewildered faces, an elderly gentleman, resplendent in best fiesta whites, offered his help and agreed to walk with us to the Camino path. He had, he told us, walked the Camino four times. As he led us away he called over to his wife who sat with friends at the nearby café. "Josefina! I'm just taking these pilgrims to put them on the right road." "Good," she replied. "While you are there could you fetch the bread?"

In Puente la Reina, sitting at the hostel in the old cobbled street leading to the bridge, thinking of the thousands of thousands of pilgrims who have walked this very street, we were joined by other pilgrims we met along the way – a random collection of walkers from Switzerland, Canada, the UK, Denmark and Holland. We had a meal together. Our conversation was not about jobs or politics but about the special qualities of the Camino and the state of our feet. When I ask one of them what is the most surprising thing about the Camino, he says, "It is this gathering, this immediate fellowship with strangers."

Kind locals and thoughtful fellow pilgrims encouraged us along the Camino with respect and care, even if some of them must also fetch the bread!

Our Father, who art in heaven,

hallowed be thy name;

thy kingdom come;

thy will be done;

on earth as it is in heaven.

Give us this day our daily bread.

And forgive us our trespasses,

as we forgive those who trespass against us.

And lead us not into temptation;

but deliver us from evil.

Amen.

Padre nuestro, que estás en el cielo,

santificado sea tu nombre;

venga a nosotros tu reino;

hágase tu voluntad;

en la tierra como en el cielo.

Danos hoy nuestro pan de cada día.

Perdona nuestras ofensas,

como también nosotros perdonamos a los que nos ofenden.

No nos dejes caer en la tentación;

y líbranos del mal.

Amén.

The Journey is the Destination

Tania Veitch
Canada

"The destination is inconsequential. The journey is home,"

Øyvind, from Norway, said to me while I hung my laundry to dry. I had voiced my fear about not making it to Santiago, given the physical problem I had developed.

What Øyvind meant is that reaching Santiago wasn't the most important part of my journey; it was the growth and the experiences along the way that mattered more; it was the journey itself.

To me the words are symbolic of how we should be living. It is easy to rush through life, focused on the destination, paying off the house, reaching retirement, making it big. But what about now? What about the journey? Do we allow ourselves the time to really enjoy the magic of this moment?

Øyvind spoke to me when we were relaxing in an albergue in Castrojeriz. There were still another 470 kilometres to walk before I would reach Santiago. We spoke for only two hours along my thirty-one-day journey, but his words were the most important thing said to me along the way. It was a rare treasure; wisdom from the lips of a pilgrim who has walked this road many times.

It seems like it is only when we are forced to slow down that we are more aware of the gifts in our lives. It is then that we truly notice what we have around us. We finally comprehend the beauty and magic of this world and the miracle of our very existence in it.

I became liberated along this ancient path. My shin splint gave me what I needed. It forced me to slow down and open my eyes. My journey became more spiritual. I learned to let go of expectations and accept the gift of the present moment.

Øyvind's words continue to play through my mind each day along my journey through life. They remind me to walk slowly, take a deep breath, smell the flowers and take notice of the little things.

My challenge became a blessing. The challenges you face along the way may be a blessing too. Look for the light being offered through the challenge and move forward with it. I truly believe the Camino gives us what we need.

Destinations are just pauses on the journey of life. We only stop to rest so that we can continue on. There is no final step, only the next stride forward on the great adventure.
Anonymous

Giving and Receiving

Liz and
Dick Crean
England

Walking the Camino de Invierno between A Rúa and Quiroga, we found ourselves in a thickly wooded valley.

We spotted an isolated water mill on the far side of the river and Lizzy remarked that, according to the guidebook, a friendly countryman called Casimiro lived there. We shouted, "¿Aún vive aqui Casimiro?" To our surprise an agile man came down from the roof where he had been working and came over to welcome us. He invited us to join him in a glass of wine. We sat down outside his house while Casimiro and his wife, Mercedes, both eighty-nine years of age, served us. The correct etiquette in this situation requires the visitor to hold the glass of wine up to the light, to remark on its clarity and colour, to sniff it approvingly and finally to down it with an appreciative exclamation, either in Spanish or simply with a sigh. We clearly passed this test because next out was the orujo, a generic word in Spanish for liqueur. Maybe it was the effect of the wine, but despite our display of reluctance ("Oh, but we can't possibly!"), Casimiro's orujo was superb. Next came licor de café, which I had to sample twice in order to fully appreciate the complex blend of coffee and alcohol. Meanwhile Mercedes had produced a large leg of jamón serrano (their own), which Casimiro began slicing with an enormous sharp knife. We were all getting on famously and I was busy thinking how we could repay this kindness when, suddenly, I realised just how we could. Casimiro had lived in that very house his entire life, staying in one place whilst his visitors were always on the move. He told me that a few years ago he had sold off the cows and that he and Mercedes very much missed the milk and cheese. "Well, that's it," I thought. "We've got a big chunk of cheese and some tomatoes." That proved a good exchange. We were left with the vision of two people for whom life is not about getting but simply about giving.

Give, and there will be gifts for you: a full measure, pressed down, shaken together, and running over, will be poured into your lap; because the amount you measure out is the amount you will be given back. Luke 6:38

Forgiveness

Rebekah Scott

Spain

I stepped into a wet morning. My socks were already damp. Within a few paces my boots had sucked up the puddles and filled with water.

Many miles and months before, I'd bought good-quality hiking boots. I'd sprayed them with water-proofer and broken them in before I left for my Camino. They were dry, comfortable, and formed to my feet, the best boots ever.

And one dark morning in Cizur Menor, just a few days in, someone took them. The thief left these boots in their place. They looked just like mine – same make, model, size and colour – but they'd seen many more miles.

They fit, though. I walked in them. No blisters, but they leaked when it rained. I hated those boots, and I hated the lowdown thief who took mine from me. I knew it could have been a mistake, but it was so much more piquant, thinking someone had deliberately done me wrong. I did not let it spoil my Camino, but every time it rained, rage squelched with every step.

Two weeks later, at a pub in Triacastela, I found my stolen boots, tied to the pack of a battered peregrina. Rage rose up in me, I felt my face go red. I swallowed hard. I had to say something... but what?

"Nice shoes," the woman said drily, looking at my feet. Her accent was German.

"You think?" I answered. "I had another pair, back by Pamplona, but now I have these ones. Someone stole my good ones, and left me their old ones. They leak."

"Someone took my good boots, too," the woman said, standing up stiffly. "I walked all the way from Dortmund in them, they were like friends. These don't leak, but they make my feet hot." She looked into my face. I looked at her. "I don't mean to, but I have your boots," she said.

"And I have yours."

We traded. I felt embarrassed. "I've hated you for days," I told her. "I'm really sorry."

The woman waved that away. Her boots were dripping wet, but she smiled and sighed as she slipped her feet inside. "No matter. I thought they were lost, and now I have them again," she said. "Thanks for bringing them back to me."

Be friends with one another, and kind, forgiving each other as readily as God forgave you in Christ. Ephesians 4:32

The Dance

Martha Crites and Jim Limardi
United States of America

Martha: I grew up in the American Midwest where people are stoic. We rarely cry. Why, then, does the Camino bring tears to my eyes? Seven years after my first pilgrimage, I am still moved unexpectedly. This morning I was listening to Galician bagpiper Carlos Núñez playing *Marcha do Entrelazado de Allariz*. I cried again. It's based on a traditional dance and roughly means "Interlaced March". The music perfectly describes what it means to walk the Camino with my husband, Jim. Our walks are interlinked, but not the same. We walk separately because my pace is faster. I love the early mornings, with the sun coming up behind me, for praying the rosary and reflecting in silence. I wait at crossroads to make sure we take the same turn. We come together at meals and the end of the day to report our experiences.

I love walking and volunteering on the Camino with Jim because I get to see him at his best: encouraging others on the trail, or tending pilgrims' feet as a hospitalero. Pilgrimage developed his bent for service. It called me into leadership; I returned to begin American Pilgrims on the Camino's first local chapter and later joined the board of directors. Our Camino at home continues like that dance; we move apart and come together.

Jim: Martha sees our Camino as a dance and she's right, a dance of kindness between us and others. I try to begin each day on the Camino expecting nothing, hoping it will be filled with what is before me, often nothing more than the stones beneath my feet. I miss many yellow arrows. I could miss Galicia altogether. Martha, however, is always there when the way veers, slowing her pace to guide me, a kindness I reciprocate by leading her down steep descents. Two kindnesses, among many, we extend to each other. Compassion begets compassion, and leads us over time, both as pilgrims and as hospitaleros, to follow the wisdom of the Spanish proverb, "Haz bien y no mires a quien" – Do good to all alike.

The rhythm of our comings and goings, these kindnesses, has become second nature to us now, like breathing, allowing us to be ourselves, yet more than ourselves. Could each of us walk the Camino alone? Probably. But the steps of this dance bring us so much joy.

> *Love is always patient and kind;*
> *it is never jealous;*
> *love is never boastful or conceited;*
> *it is never rude or selfish;*
> *it does not take offence,*
> *and is not resentful.*
> *Love takes no pleasure in other people's sins*
> *but delights in the truth;*
> *it is always ready to excuse, to trust,*
> *to hope and to endure whatever comes.*
> *Love does not come to an end.*

1 Corinthians 13:4–8

Coincidences

Sam Pinkerton
Australia

One morning in the albergue about a week after I started out I noticed a stranger near the door. As other pilgrims prepared to leave he sat on his bunk looking in my direction.

Preparing my feet for another day took time, and I was nearly the last to leave the hostel. As I put my pack on and moved slowly towards the door, the stranger's attention was clearly focused on my uncomfortable limp. I was passing by when he said in a thick accent, laced with mystery, "We Spanish say that on the Camino, blisters are our sins working their way from the body."

I thought to myself, "Yeah, that really helps," and said, "Thanks," dismissively. What did I care? I would never see him again.

That morning I walked slowly and in solitude, quite desperately trying to distract myself from the pain in my feet. My thoughts kept returning to my chance encounter with this mysterious Spaniard. A feeling of remorse began to overwhelm me, remorse I suppose for an opportunity lost. Should I have engaged that messenger and listened more intently? As I walked with his words in my mind I was beginning to truly believe that the blisters on my feet were there as penance for my sins.

It was many days later, when my feet blisters had healed and calluses had grown, that I rested upon a wall and saw a distant figure hobbling in pain along the dirt path. As he came towards me I eventually saw that this was actually the mysterious Spaniard.

Inspired by the coincidence, I said wisely, "It seems your sins are working their way from your body."

Carl Jung called coincidences like this "synchronicity" and intimated that by stopping to ponder these occurrences we will begin to see direct evidence of a divine force involved in our lives.

The Spaniard's eyes lit up and he held aloft a seer's finger. "You know, we Spanish say that on the Camino, blisters are our sins working their way from the body!"

In that moment I realised he had not the slightest idea who I was.

Fr Augusto Losada Lopez, the priest in Triacastela, instructed us pilgrims to be kind to ourselves and to be joyous in our lives as a "penance" for any sins. But it's Fr Augusto's final words of the Mass that are the ones that resonate: "Remember God doesn't count your steps or Santiago weigh your pack – what they measure is your heart, pilgrim, so look to your heart ... and take care of your feet!" Nell, Ireland

Lesley
Rankin
Ireland

Nothing can be Loved at Speed

Lead, kindly light, amid the encircling gloom,
lead thou me on.
The night is dark, and I am far from home,
lead thou me on.
Keep thou my feet; I do not ask to see
the distant scene, one step enough for me.

John Henry Newman

On my first Camino, the last two lines of the first verse of this magnificent hymn kept reverberating in my head, and ever since then I have used them as my daily prayer as I walk.

The beauty of any Camino is that you learn to live in the present, to abandon past regrets and fear of what the future may have in store. This gives you time for self-discovery and delight in the here and now, for the joy of companionship and/or solitude. There is time to notice tiny signs of life: a goldfinch in a field of ripening wheat; a highly organised trail of ants, each carrying a load as large as itself over vast distances; an early-morning frogs' chorus, emanating from a misty pond.

In the words of the Australian poet Michael Leunig:

O God our Father,

We pray for another way of being, another way of knowing.

Across the difficult terrain of our existence we have attempted to build a highway and in doing so we have lost our footpath.

God lead us to our footpath where we may move at the speed of natural creatures and feel the earth's love beneath our feet. Lead us where step by step we may feel the movement of creation in our hearts.

We give you thanks for places of simplicity and peace. Let us find such a place within ourselves.

We give thanks for places of refuge and beauty. Let us find such a place within ourselves.

We give thanks for places of nature's truth and freedom, of joy, inspiration and renewal, places where all creatures may find acceptance and belonging. Let us search for these places in the world, in ourselves and in others. Let us restore them. Let us strengthen and protect them and let us create them.

May we always remember that nothing can be loved at speed.

God lead us to the slow path; to the joyous insights of the pilgrim; another way of knowing; another way of being. Amen.

Life Changing

Barry Brooks
United States of America

A few years back at Christmas one of my co-workers gave me a plate with my family crest. The crest has three scallop shells. I found out that the shell is the symbol for a pilgrimage in Spain called the Way of Saint James, the Camino de Santiago.

I told myself I was going to walk the Way one day just as my ancestors did. But I soon forgot about it and life went on. As the years went by the idea kept surfacing from time to time. Then one day I found myself with the time and means to go. I had no idea what to expect or why I was doing this... Mid-life crisis? A desire for one great adventure? Escape from the daily grind? I somehow felt compelled. I *had* to do this! What a wonderful, magical and spiritual experience it became. Like any adventure or journey which involves physical and emotional endurance, you experience a bond with the people you experience it with. During my walk into Burgos I walked with a woman. We only walked together for one day but the connection was made! After parting ways we started emailing, and well, one thing led to another and now I live in Barcelona and will soon be married to the love of my life. Gracias Santiago!

After I arrived I sat in the Cathedral of Santiago and thought: *Man, do my feet hurt!*

It has been an amazing journey and exceeded all expectations. I remembered back to the third day when I stopped at a church and met a nun who gave me a copy of the pilgrim beatitudes, the gist of which is that we are here to care for one another and the Camino begins after you leave Santiago. We are all pilgrims in life. We do not need much but we need each other. That was, I think, the biggest surprise for me. I thought this was going to be a solitary journey. But the opposite happened. The Camino will always be in my heart.

Blessed are you, pilgrim, if you discover that the Camino opens your eyes to the unseen.

Blessed are you, pilgrim, if you are not so much concerned about arriving, but arriving with the others.

Blessed are you, pilgrim, if you discover the Camino is filled with names and sunrises.

Blessed are you, pilgrim, if you find out that the Camino begins where it ends.

Blessed are you, pilgrim, if your backpack empties of things and your heart does not know where to fit so many emotions.

Blessed are you, pilgrim, if you understand that a step back to help someone is worth a thousand steps forward.

Blessed are you, pilgrim, if you don't have enough thanks for all that surprises you on the Way.

Blessed are you, pilgrim, if you look for the truth and make of your Camino a life in search of what is the Way, the Truth, and the Life.

Blessed are you, pilgrim, if on your way you meet yourself and give yourself all the time in the world not to neglect what is in your heart.

Blessed are you, pilgrim, if you discover that the Camino is a lot about silence; and silence, about prayer; and prayer, about the encounter with God who is waiting for you. Anonymous

Gifts

Alan Pearce
Australia

During my first Camino I stayed in the albergue in Astorga. The young, very efficient hospitalera was from Canada. I am a sucker for people's stories, so I inquired why she was there.

Jessica had been an exchange student in Madrid from her university in Canada. She mastered Spanish, and decided to try this thing called the "Camino". She did no training or preparation. One day she hobbled into the Astorga albergue crippled with blisters, sopping wet because it was raining heavily and she had no wet weather gear, and broke because the ATMs would not accept her credit card.

The hospitalero asked if he could help and she said she "burst into floods of tears". When he asked her what was wrong she said that she had no money. He said she could stay for free. She said that she could not walk because of the blisters. He said she could stay until they were healed. So she did.

When I arrived she had been there for about a week. The blisters were healed, and her credit card was working again. Her biggest problem was what to say to her father who, because she had missed her flight back to Canada, kept ringing her to ask when she was going home. As a father myself I thought this was a very fair question and asked her the same. I will never forget her reply: "I came in here with nothing," she said, "and the Camino gave me everything I needed unconditionally. I cannot leave until I pay it back."

Some years later I became very ill myself and it seemed that I would not be able to travel again. That changed when slowly the treatment began to work, but I asked myself: "What would I have most regretted *not* doing if I had not been able to travel in the future?" The answer was: "Not giving something back to the Camino." I wondered, "How can I do that?"

Following Jessica's inspiration and example, I have been a hospitalero three times, and again next year. Thanks, Jess, for everything.

For I was hungry and you gave me food; I was thirsty and you gave me drink; I was a stranger and you made me welcome. Matthew 25:35

Forty Years of Pilgrimage and Service

Marion Marples
United Kingdom

I still don't know why my friend Jane and I signed up for an evening course on Gothic Architecture on top of our existing studies. But amongst other things, we learnt for the first time about the medieval pilgrimage route to Santiago. Full of enthusiasm, we applied for a student travel grant, studied the only book on the subject in the University Library (*The Great Pilgrimage of the Middle Ages* by Vera and Helmut Hell) and set off for France. I was used to walking but Jane was not and soon we could not manage to carry the tent and walk the footpaths as planned. So we took public transport to visit the fabulous Romanesque churches in Poitiers, Melle, Aulnay and Saintes with their fantastic carvings.

As we reached the Pyrenees we were running low on money. At that time it took two hours to arrange a phone call to England, so we sent a telegram to my mother, requesting funds. We camped for five days in Saint-Jean-Pied-de-Port, and lived off home-made onion soup until £5 finally arrived. Then we were able to walk to Valcarlos and catch an early bus to Pamplona before making our way home.

All this was in 1972. Had we actually reached Santiago we would have joined the six other pilgrims who were awarded Compostelas that year. But we had no idea of the size of France or Spain, or any information on how to undertake such a journey. We certainly had no idea of it being a personal pilgrimage or any concept of St James.

In 1983, now married with a small son, my attention was drawn to a meeting to be held at St James's, Piccadilly for people with an interest in the pilgrimage to Santiago de Compostela. I immediately signed up. We organised Practical Pilgrim Days, lectures and visits. Membership grew quickly and we explored places like Reading Abbey, Herefordshire churches and St James

the Great, Stoke Orchard with its unique twelfth-century wall paintings telling the life of St James.

In 1993 we took part in the first English pilgrimage along the Camino Inglés since the Reformation and in 1994 we joined a French organised pilgrimage across the Pyrenees from Bayonne to Pamplona by the Baztan route.

In 1995 I became Secretary of the Confraternity of Saint James (CSJ). I worked from home but it became so busy we had to find an office. With the prospect of a Holy Year in 1999, in which the Xunta de Galicia were investing heavily, I realised I could no longer rely on the information learnt from others about the pilgrimage, and in 1998 I decided I had to do it myself in order to be able to speak authentically. I took seven weeks' leave of absence from my teaching job. Having arrived in Pamplona on foot in 1994, I decided I would start there. I arrived in Santiago thirty-seven days later. Although I did not know it at the time, this pilgrimage prepared me to be able to leave teaching, work more days for the CSJ and make other important changes in my life.

After the millennium I walked with a group from Southwark and St Albans Cathedrals from Winchester to Portsmouth and in weekly instalments over ten years through western France, eventually picking up on my earlier "Paris" route in Melle. In 2010, having pretty well covered the miles between London and Santiago, I arrived back at Saint-Jean-Pied-de-Port, which was now thronging with pilgrims.

In the 1980s and 1990s most people did not really know what a pilgrimage was. But with many accounts of walking and cycling being published and with word-of-mouth enthusiasm as the number of pilgrims increased, more people found out about the pilgrimage. Gradually people spoke and wrote more of the inner, spiritual journey as well as the physical, of the transformation of heart and mind that becomes possible. Nowadays, with so much advice and support available on the internet, it can be hard to appreciate the pioneering work of the writers of our guide who needed to walk each route several times while compiling all the information first hand. Now, with so many albergues, we should not forget the pioneering initiatives such as the development of the Refugio Gaucelmo.

So what has changed? Yes, there are problems of scale and overcrowding, although the amount of accommodation and the number of routes and guidebooks grows each year. Yes, people find Santiago too crowded. With so many pilgrims from around the world there can be friction between pilgrims and local people due to language difficulties and lack of consideration.

But the enduring experience of the Camino is of the joy of simplicity, of friendship, shared experience and struggle, of transformation and the desire for a new kind of living and being.

Each one of you has received a special grace, so, like good stewards responsible for all these different graces of God, put yourself at the service of others. 1 Peter 4:10

Statue of Constantine – Church of Sainte-Hilaire, Melle

Marion Marples has retired after 26 years' service as the Secretary of the Confraternity of Saint James. Members and pilgrims from around the world would like to thank her for her huge contribution to the Camino to Santiago. We hope that her own pilgrimage continues for many years to come.

Pilgrim Angels

Blanche Malankowski-Smith, Ben Smith and Colleen Smith

United States of America

The Pilgrim Angels, that's what I called them. They were everywhere from Roncesvalles to Santiago, walking with us, meeting us along the way, sharing food, filling water bottles at a fountain. When they appeared it was often unexpected. Walking the Camino with my blind husband and adult daughter, I didn't imagine that the "angels" would be the ones who would settle in my soul and connect me to this Camino.

On the first day we missed a yellow arrow on a wall. A child stopped us and pointed out the way. Just after Pamplona we were lost. My husband asked an elderly gentleman for help. He led us back along boulevards, intersecting streets and side alleys to the albergue. At the door he said, "If they are full, you can stay in my home." Then he waited until he knew all was well and vanished. Trekking up the mountain to Alto del Perdón, we met two young Korean women who gave us chocolate. We shared stories of our visit to Korea. There was Susie, from Hungary, who suddenly hugged me one morning saying, "I have so much respect for you," and began to cry. I was touched. Susie came back to us later through a message left under a rock. We never noticed the note, but Yvonne from Britain whom we had chatted with days before saw it peeking out from the rock and took it with her. Then she met us. "Being nosy I just had to read it," she said, "and now I get to deliver it."

Books could be written about these angels – such as seventy-six-year-old Jean Claude on his sixth pilgrimage who helped my husband when he fell. In Foncebadón, all the pilgrims at dinner offered their salads to my daughter, who is gluten intolerant, when they realised she wasn't able to eat the pasta. Sven slept on the cold church floor with us that evening and then walked my husband down the hill.

The "angels" are there. They walk with you. They talk to you. They eat with you. They sleep with you. Everyone walking in the same direction. Everyone greeting you with, "Buen Camino."

"Pilgrim with guardian angel" – stained glass in Tosantos albergue

I myself will send an angel before you to guard you as you go and bring you to the place that I have prepared. Exodus 23:20

Scallop Shell

Gerry Riordan
Ireland

I have walked the Camino three times, twice with my brother and once with my seventeen-year-old daughter. I have found it often tough, sometimes exhilarating, never boring.

Great moments have included:

The first beer after walking 30 kilometres – magic.

Walking into an unfolding Spanish dawn – awe-inspiring.

Arriving in Samos, by luck on Corpus Christi, and joining the monks on their procession through the monastery while they sang Gregorian chant – awesome.

Having shared experiences and bonding with my daughter – brilliant.

I have brought back three pilgrim shells from my Caminos:

One I lost.

One I gave to a friend of mine who was suffering from cancer. Later, after he recovered, he gave it back to me. He told me the gesture had meant a huge amount to him.

One I hung on my parents' gravestone in Balla, County Mayo. Balla was an old pilgrimage centre where pilgrims gathered to start their pilgrimage to Croagh Patrick.

I will start my next Camino from there this September, walking to Croagh Patrick and from there on to Saint-Jean and the Camino Francés to Santiago.

Why has the Camino captured my imagination and become part of my life?

I am not a religious person – quite the opposite – so this is something that has taken me by surprise and puzzled me.

On reflection it seems to me that the Camino has become more than the sum of its parts.

Its parts are easy to see:

Walking in fresh air in beautiful countryside.

Meeting and sharing your journey with interesting people.

Leaving your worldly concerns behind and just walking.

And yet I have found that there is something more, something that caused me to give the pilgrim shell to a sick friend, or hang it on my parents' grave.

This something might be called spirituality.

Give me my scallop-shell of quiet, my staff of faith to walk upon,

my scrip of joy, immortal diet, my bottle of salvation,

my gown of glory, hope's true gage, and thus I'll take my pilgrimage.

Sir Walter Raleigh

Companions on the Way

Liz Thackwray
England

The image from Micah of acting justly and with kindness came to me on the first evening at dinner. There I met some of the companions I was to walk with over the next two weeks. Their first gifts were practical – someone happy to book a bed for the next day for those of us without a phone, others able to translate from French into one of many languages present. As the days passed we also discovered who was good at first aid and who had the uncanny knack of finding food or water first.

By the end of the first week there was a group of about ten of us walking at different paces but arriving each afternoon at the same place. The practical help, awareness and friendship gave a uniqueness and shape to all our journeys. The mutual support, friendship and reassurance were remarked upon more than once, and several were surprised we had only met one another in the past few days. Our new community, albeit temporary, had gelled in a profound way.

We all gave and received something. On our last evening we reflected on our time together. We found that those of us who had already walked to Santiago had given the others a reassurance that they too could complete their journeys. Someone else noted that, like life, there would be good days as well as difficult ones. Another said that the opportunity to walk the Camino was something that should not be rushed; it was a special space. We also shared more humorous memories; the impromptu musical evening; and the cooking and eating of some very convivial evening meals.

What did I take away? I realised this special community in a short space of time had shown me companions were all around. That being alongside one another encompassed both giving and receiving practical help, friendship and support. I resolved I would try to continue practising this in my daily life.

This is what the Lord asks of you: only this, to act justly, to love tenderly and to walk humbly with your God. Micah 6:8

Community

Mary and Albert Cutts
United Kingdom

We joined the Confraternity of Saint James. We bought lightweight, quick-dry clothing. We studied the guidebooks and we cut out the relevant pages. We worked hard on reducing our backpack weight. We prayed. We prepared.

But on day one the Chemin threw up the unexpected. In the half-light of early morning we joined the group of departing pilgrims for Mass in the magnificent cathedral of Le Puy. Afterwards the priest gathered us round a statue of St James. We were invited to write out a prayer, place it in a basket and take another's to carry with us. The priest told us that we had joined a community, that we were now a family – we would walk and talk with each other, eat together, lodge together, and our paths would cross frequently in the coming weeks.

We left the cathedral – descending the impressive stairs down the hill onto the Rue St Jacques and out of the town, following the red and white balises which were to guide us step by step all the way to the Pyrenees. A dramatic departure. We walked out of Le Puy up the steep hill on towards Monistrol, where we fell into step with our neighbours and, as we exchanged hopes and fears, we suddenly had an inkling that the priest's words might have been prophetic. And so it was to be. For the next weeks we travelled in the knowledge and deep-down feeling that we were part of a thousand years of pilgrim walkers – starting with that epoch-making journey when Godescalc, Bishop of Le Puy, set out in AD 950. We made friends, we shared so many experiences, we did feel part of a family. This was something our initial preparations had not prepared us for – the intense community aspect of the Camino. It was so much more than a physical and spiritual journey. It was a journey of people, camaraderie and friendships.

50

Let us be concerned for each other, to stir a response in love and good works. Do not stay away from the meetings of the community, as some do, but encourage each other to go; the more so as you see the Day drawing nearer.
Hebrews 10:24–25

A Journey of Peace and Trust

Andrée Lombard
South Africa

My Camino, truly a journey of peace and trust in the Lord. A time for reflection crossing mountains and valleys, through forests, open fields and delightful villages.

Plenty of cows, horses, sheep – but few people in central France. On day one, a man on a bicycle, a man on a horse, no one else! The actual path was sometimes rocky, sometimes muddy with enormous puddles to avoid; sometimes the path was only a foot wide through grass higher than my head! A walk of silent prayer and songs of praise.

My constant prayer...

"Be still and know that I am God,

Be still and know that I am God,

I am the Lord who 'leadeth' thee,

In you, O Lord, do I put my trust..."

All along the way there are signs – red and white, then yellow and white, orange, red and yellow... But always the small stylised shell, a yellow symbol on a blue background, high up in the trees. To me little candles, lights of Christ here and there to guide the way. Without them it is impossible to walk this path and I thank God for guiding me safely and sending kind companions and people to help.

How I needed God's help – I lost my mobile charger, and lo and behold in the next ancient town there was a modern mobile shop right on the path, open on a Monday afternoon when all shops in France are usually closed. When I needed an optician to repair my glasses – at the next town there was one!

A special time was when a hospitalero accompanied me to the top of a mountain to a beautiful church. Inside he sang the pilgrims' song – "Ultrea", "God is with us". A moving, tearful moment!

When I injured my leg and was unable to walk – God sent many angels to help, and with their help and loving care I recovered.

Thank you, Jesus, for a most amazing time and amazing people.

Let the morning bring me word of your unfailing love
for I have put my trust in you. Show me the way I should go,
for to you I lift up my soul.

Psalm 143:8

Dedication

Daniel Lynch

Ireland

I first heard about the Camino a couple of months after my partner Mark died suddenly. Tony, our local priest, was going to take a group. It didn't sound a bit enjoyable even though he insisted it would do me the world of good. So to see what it was like I agreed to go out to Spain with him to book the accommodation for the group. When I saw the distances involved between the albergues I thought, "I won't be doing the Camino!"

But back home I thought about it constantly and when they offered me a place with the group of twenty-one, I hesitantly agreed to go. I decided to walk the Camino for Mark.

When I first met the group it was strange. All different characters and a big difference in ages. At twenty-two, I was one of the youngest. As I began to get to know the others I discovered they were kind, funny and caring people. I began to feel comfortable and helped them along the way every way I could, whether it was singing to get the group motivated or just being a listening ear for people as they were for me. One of my best memories of the Camino was a day when we all walked by ourselves. It got me thinking of what an amazing experience this actually was. I was proud to be doing this for someone I loved. I began to notice that I woke up in good humour ready for another day's walking. Something I hadn't felt for months.

On the last day of walking it all became very emotional. We sang all the way to the end. It was absolutely brilliant, an amazing experience, one of the best things I ever did in my life. I met the best of friends while doing this. I came home with a big weight off my shoulders and I hope to walk the Camino again in the near future.

And I will ask the Father, and he shall give you another Comforter, that he may be with you for ever. John 14:16

Helpful Hallucination

Lydia Gillen
Ireland

The hospitalero in Grañon said that the albergues in Tosantos and Atapuerca were "muy bonita" [very pretty]. Leaving Tosantos, I was determined to go as far as Atapuerca that night. But it was Sunday and I didn't start until after Mass in Epinosa.

Departing St Juan de Ortega, I had no worries. The path lay through forests. But the trees on the south side of the track had been cut back so I had to walk in the heat of the afternoon sun. It was nearly six when I saw Atapuerca; with relief I drank my last 100 millilitres of water. But when I got to the church I was told that the albergue was closed. I went to a nearby private albergue but it was full. I returned into the village and met two little boys about four and six years of age cycling on wide-handled bikes. I asked if they knew of an albergue. They told me to follow them. They brought me on a circuitous route back up to where I had been. I asked if they knew anywhere else and again they told me to follow them.

I began to get very anxious. I had no food because I had been coming to a "shared meal". Would I get a bed, or, more importantly, a roof over my head? Exhausted, I began to cry. Suddenly, out in front of me I saw two big yellow arrows moving slowly ahead. I said, "Lord, I know I am hungry and thirsty and tired, but surely I am not so far gone as to be hallucinating?" I looked again and those yellow arrows were still there. I could not believe what I was seeing. I wiped my hand across my eyes and those yellow arrows were actually the two little boys wearing yellow T-shirts and riding their wide-handled bikes! The utter relief! It was like God our Father was leaning out of heaven chuckling and saying, "Lydia, when will you learn to trust me?" I found the albergue and I did get a bed!

*Be strong and courageous. Do not be afraid;
do not be discouraged, for the Lord your God
will be with you wherever you go.* Joshua 1:9

Together

Susan
Spencer
and
Michelle
Herring
United States of America

I wanted to walk the Camino to Santiago for fifteen years. Even though I didn't know it at the time, I was waiting for my daughter, Michelle, to be old enough to walk it with me. But she almost didn't. The first time I asked her she said, "Why on earth would anyone ever wanna do that?" But a little bit later in the year she brought it up again on my visit to see her in New York: "Mom, I think we should do the Camino after all." The time was finally right for both of us for our own separate reasons. We wondered: what would this be like for the two of us? We are mother and daughter, with such an age difference, and in such different stages of our lives. She was twenty and I was fifty-nine. What if one became injured or ill? Would we become closer than we already were or would we end up not liking each other?

And then we walked. Every day for thirty-five days. Together. We talked, we laughed, we hurt, we sang, we were silent. Every day we faced highs and lows, both emotionally and geographically, in this crazy adventure. Together. We let each day unfold and never did we think about walking without each other. Even through the aches and the pains and the blisters (oh, my daughter's poor blisters!), we were able to say at the end of each day that we were fed, sheltered and OK. We walked every step together until we reached Santiago. And guess what: we still loved each other when we got there. In fact, we felt closer than ever. There was a strength and determination that the two of us saw in each other that amazed us both, and we revelled in the lessons we learned from both the Way and each other. Even though we walked five hundred miles as two bodies, we walked into Santiago as one spirit. Together.

Better two than one, for thus their work is really profitable. If one should fall, the other helps them up. Ecclesiastes 4:9–10

Lost and Found

Trevor Hockey
United Kingdom

I was lost, and that must have been obvious to the guy who asked me if I needed help. He led me to the office of a church in Irun, where I received a credencial and my first sello (seal). Afterwards at a junction he showed me a yellow arrow: "Follow them and you will be OK. Look out for the one I painted." Then, "Buen camino."

I am so grateful to that "amigo" for setting me on my way.

I walked mostly by myself throughout March guided by the yellow arrows. I frequently felt companionship from footprints made by those who had walked before and, strangely, from those who would follow. At the end of the day I would sometimes be alone in the albergue, but most times there would be other pilgrims. We shared the same experience, we arrived tired and hungry, together we ate and slept. In the morning, refreshed, we left at our own pace and made our way west to Santiago and maybe beyond.

Amazing Grace, how sweet the sound
that saved a wretch like me.
I once was lost but now am found,
was blind, but now I see.

'Twas Grace that taught my heart to fear
and Grace my fears relieved.
How precious did that Grace appear
the hour I first believed.

Through many dangers, toils and snares
I have already come;
'tis Grace has brought me safe thus far
and Grace will lead me home.

The Lord has promised good to me.
His word my hope secures.
He will my shield and portion be
as long as life endures.

Yes, when this flesh and heart shall fail,
and mortal life shall cease,
I shall possess within the veil,
a life of joy and peace.
John Newton

Friends Forever

Frank
Burns
Scotland

I first visited Santiago de Compostela when I took a detour on my journey to Lourdes. I was inspired by the many pilgrims I encountered and so resolved to come back as a pilgrim on the Camino.

In the ensuing seven years, with a group of four or five lifelong friends, I have walked different parts of the various Camino routes to Santiago. Our friendship goes back almost fifty years to our schooldays at the Jesuit St Aloysius' College in Glasgow, Scotland.

One of the questions I am asked is whether I find the Camino a religious or even a spiritual experience. For some reason, apart from those times when I come across a church en route, I don't find it easy to pray in the conventional sense while walking the Camino. Perhaps it is because of the physical effort required in walking and the constant search for yellow arrows. However, I do find it profoundly spiritual, and make an effort each day to walk on my own for a while to reflect on the relationships and friendships that have sustained me over a lifetime.

As I walk the Camino and enjoy the companionship of my friends, I remember those who have also travelled with me throughout my life: my wife, my daughter and son, my sister and brothers, my parents, and other friends, especially those who have finished their life's journey ahead of me.

Two friends who started out on the Camino with us have sadly died – one of them, Hugh, passed away in Santiago immediately on completion of the Camino. It was a devastating conclusion to a week of joyful walking and celebration of friendship.

Hugh's death has left a void in our band of brothers, just as Bobby's did before him; for both of them and for ourselves we will continue to walk the Camino as long as we are fit to do so, celebrating and remembering those friendships. Amigos para siempre.

Don't walk behind me; I may not lead.
Don't walk in front of me; I may not follow.
Just walk beside me and be my friend.
Anonymous

Camino Providence

Robert Fink

Canada

While walking the Camino I met a woman from Finland. We instantly liked each other and even though I walked at a faster pace we decided to walk side by side. As we walked we began to share a little about ourselves, and why we found ourselves travelling this ancient path.

It turned out that my companion had just completed her theology studies and needed to decide whether to take the next step to be ordained into the Lutheran priesthood. This decision had been made more difficult as her husband and her teenage son strongly disagreed with her choice of vocation. Her husband did not believe in God, and her son was deeply concerned that her attention would be focused away from him.

Over several days we discussed all aspects of the future, including the potential breakup of her marriage if she continued towards ordination. She was stuck at a crossroads.

At the end of our fifth day we stopped for the night in a large town with many excellent places to eat. We decided on a place that had been recommended to us.

As we were scanning our menus and enjoying a drink, I happened to see a tall man with blond hair who looked distinctly Finnish. Without my companion's knowledge, I invited him to join us at our table. To my delight he did come from Finland, but we also found out that he had been a Lutheran priest for eighteen years and he had recently quit his day job.

I excused myself soon after finishing dinner so I could let my two friends talk about their common bond. The next morning, they were still deep in discussion. Realising that they had much more to talk about, I said that I planned to continue walking on my own that day, and said goodbye.

To this day, I have no idea how things turned out, and all I can say is that the Camino brings each of us what we need, when we need it!

You did not choose me, no, I chose you; and I commissioned you to go out and to bear fruit, fruit that will last; and then the Father will give you anything you ask him in my name.
John 15:16

Mary had a Donkey

Pauline
and Morrell
Rosseau
South Africa

Newly retired, we stood at the doors of the Cathedral
in Le Puy, excited, and wondering if we would cope
with our 1,550-kilometre pilgrimage. We learnt that problems
are seldom as bad as we imagined. The mountains, which looked
steep, and the path, which was muddy and slippery, were always
achievable. One of the first challenges was that few pilgrims in
France spoke English. We had a number of days when we felt quite
isolated and lonely, but this also created the ideal circumstances
for us to talk as a couple.

The rocky paths in France gave us an opportunity to share about
the difficult times of our school-going years; sitting on top of a
mountain reminded us of those special times of our lives, some
shared and some unique to each of us. Ascending the Alto del
Perdón, we called to mind the things for which we needed to
ask pardon, and we were sure that the steep descent must have
been the penance! Watching two butterflies dance on the path
reminded us of our mothers, both of whom had died the previous
year. We shared our happy memories and regrets, finding healing
and understanding as we did so. We were struck by the variety
of beautiful spider webs glistening with dew in the morning sun.
These led us to share about the webs which ensnare us and those we
need to avoid in these later years of our married life, like becoming
too busy, attachment to our possessions and impatience with each
other's foibles. One question we hoped to find the answer to as we
walked was: Would two be company or a crowd in our retirement?

On the Meseta, we found that the stark simplicity encouraged
deeper reflection. The interminably long, straight path challenged
our sense of humour as conversation waned and our feet burned
and blistered. We encouraged each other in our low moments with
the saying: *he walked for us so we can walk for him.* One of us then
retorted: *Yes, but Mary had a donkey!* And so humour was restored.

The blessings we experienced as a couple walking our 67-day pilgrimage reassured us that we can look forward to two being company. We had time to dream, to plan and to laugh together. One of the Camino's many gifts.

Wherever you go, I will go, wherever you live, I will live. Your people shall be my people, and your God, my God. Ruth 1:16

Walking with Nature

Michelle Courtney
Australia

When I first heard of the Camino I bought a guidebook and found myself dreaming my way through the pages. One of the few colour photographs in the book was of a poncho-clad pilgrim descending to the village of El Acebo. A decade later I was the poncho-clad pilgrim in that exact place. It was as exhilarating as I imagined.

Some say "the first day is the hardest". I think of that first day as one of the most beautiful. It is glorious to climb out of Saint-Jean-Pied-de-Port as the dawn light melts the clouds. Lacy spider webs with sparkling droplets of dew cling to fences. Up and up the road winds while daybreak colours the mountain landscape dotted with red roofs, flocks of sheep, windswept horses and fellow pilgrims. The bold blue midday sky at the mountaintop is circled by raptors. I'll always be grateful to the fellow pilgrim that first day who reminded me that "God makes us lose our breath so we will stop and appreciate the view".

Described by some as "the boring bit in the middle", to me the Meseta is a most beautiful and expansive landscape. Outside Frómista at dawn, tiny snails created parallel paths along frosty handrails. A delicate bird swayed on a wheat sheaf in the afternoon near Sahagún. Huge fields of sunflowers bowed their heads in the evening. From Alto de Mostelares, the breathtaking views in both directions of the Meseta path are never boring.

Dreaming of my first Camino, I knew that I was preparing for a spiritual pilgrimage. I didn't appreciate that being in the outdoors would contribute so profoundly to my spiritual experience. Day after new day it is wonderful to be living at a walking pace within the scenery, the weather, the phases of the moon, and the path of the sun. Each day moving closer to Santiago, to nature, to myself, to others, and to God.

In every walk with nature I receive far more than I seek. John Muir

Young Single Female

Forming friendships while on the Camino is quite different from other parts of life. The Camino is one of the few places where people do not search for commonalities such as what you do for a living and where you went to school when they first meet you. Instead, pilgrims are open to all sorts of backgrounds without judgement.

Yosmar Martinez
United States of America

This openness yielded unexpected and uncommon friendships for this youngish single woman... On each of my Caminos I became friends with farmers, blue-collar workers, octogenarians, etc. from all around the world. These friendships vary greatly from my highly educated, urban, mid-level professional social circle I have back home. Our backgrounds and lifestyles may differ but we share core values of honesty, humility and openness.

In addition, I felt oddly safe with people who were so different from me. Thanks to social media and the ease of travel, I've managed to keep in touch with many of the friends I have developed in my four Caminos. In addition, many of these friendships have had ripple effects I could have never imagined. A pilgrim I met early on during my first Camino happened to mention the pilgrim association here in the United States, American Pilgrims on the Camino (APOC). Upon returning from my first Camino, I became a member of this wonderful organisation and continued creating amazing friendships. Once again, many of these people have drastically different backgrounds from me but they share common views of humanity and the world. They also value the Camino experience as much as I do. These friends continue having an impact on me. Many have helped me plan future Caminos. Others have allowed me to tag along on their Caminos. An unexpected number of them have volunteered in many capacities to help me with an upcoming Camino cookbook that reflects my love for all the foods of the Camino.

Finally, many have allowed me to pay it forward and help them with their future Caminos.

I would rather walk with a friend in the dark, than alone in the light. Helen Keller

Room for Everyone

John Rafferty
From Scotland, living in Spain

By the time we reached Santiago we had met people of all ages from many different countries. We also met: those who had prepared and those who hadn't, people with huge rucksacks and those with almost nothing in their packs, people who were shy and those who were outgoing, pilgrims who believed in God and those who didn't, people who were happy and people who were sad, people who had changed their lives and others who were happy with life the way it is. We met people who had lost partners and couples walking with their children. We met those who had experienced broken hearts and many who were falling in love with life.

We all walked the same road and when we got to Santiago Cathedral there was a place for each of us. Every one.

I wrote these words after my very first pilgrimage to Santiago. When I set out from Seville there were no other pilgrims on the way and I spoke no English, and it remained this way until I reached Salamanca nineteen days later. But the people were kind to me, shepherds waved from the hills and I enjoyed the solitude. It was cold in the early mornings but by lunchtime I had to put on sunscreen. It was like walking through the seasons.

After Salamanca a friend joined me and we encountered more pilgrims. One or two at first, then a steady stream. We were all different, yet we were all walking in the same direction.

We walked into the Plaza Obradoiro elated. We hugged and kissed and threw off our rucksacks. The joy was mixed with sadness because soon we would part. Each of us would go our separate ways to rejoin our lives at home. There was a time to be together and a time to part.

Together we mounted the steps to the great Cathedral and when we got inside there was a place for each of us. Every one.

There is a season for everything, a time for every occupation under heaven:

A time for giving birth, a time for dying; a time for planting, a time for uprooting what has been planted.

A time for killing, a time for healing; a time for knocking down, a time for building.

A time for tears, a time for laughter; a time for mourning, a time for dancing.

A time for throwing stones away, a time for gathering them up;

A time for embracing, a time to refrain from embracing.

A time for searching, a time for losing; a time for keeping, a time for throwing away.

A time for tearing, a time for sewing; a time for keeping silent, a time for speaking.

A time for loving, a time for hating; a time for war; a time for peace.

Ecclesiastes 3:1–8

The End and the Beginning

Kenneil Mitchell
United States of America

Is this the end? It felt so long ago that I started walking the Vía de la Plata in Mérida with my professor and classmates. I'm standing near the lighthouse at Finisterre, the End of the World, watching the sunset painting the sky a multitude of colours. While looking at the ocean, I started thinking about what I have achieved on this pilgrimage.

One achievement is talking to other pilgrims from different countries who speak languages other than English. Not knowing how to speak different languages can cause some people to distance themselves from conversation with other pilgrims. This is often the case in America, where people can be quick to judge another person just because they don't speak the same language as them. This wasn't the case on the Camino as I found myself having different conversations with different pilgrims who spoke a variety of languages. It opened my eyes to how diverse the Camino truly is and how everyone is the same on this trail.

Another more personal achievement is that I have gained the ability to trust in myself more to overcome life's challenges. There have been many times on the Camino where I doubted who I truly was because I lost my group or lost my way. I'm hard on myself because at twenty-one I'm the youngest in my family out of three brothers and seven sisters. I'm the only son to graduate high school and go to college. Because of the pressure that I put on myself, I thrive on being a perfectionist in any activity I do. That has made me more demanding of myself and I know that in doing the Camino, I needed to let that go. I needed to learn to trust in myself in order to keep going to my destination.

But now I'm here at the end, at Finisterre. The overall experience has been challenging but emotionally fulfilling. Coming from a big family in the small town of Columbia in South Carolina, there's a lot of pressure on me to make a difference. Looking at the ocean, I knew that this is not the end. In many ways my Camino is just beginning, as I continue to challenge myself to become a happier and better person.

In the Bible (Revelation 1:8) we read: "'I am the Alpha and the Omega – the beginning and the end,' says the Lord God."

However, in the façade of the Cathedral of Santiago, there is a carving in which the Alpha and Omega are reversed: Omega and Alpha. Nowhere else in the Christian world are the symbols reversed. The message is clear at this end of the Camino to Santiago. It is the end and the beginning.

American Pilgrims on the Camino

Congratulations from American Pilgrims on the Camino on the publication of *Camino to Santiago*. Congratulations also to all our fellow pilgrims who are reading it in preparation for, or remembrance of, the journey.

Our mission as American Pilgrims on the Camino is to foster the enduring tradition of the Camino by supporting its infrastructure, by gathering pilgrims together, and by providing information and encouragement to past and future pilgrims.

With more than 2,000 members and an all-volunteer board of directors, we hold an annual National Gathering and regular meetings of our more than 30 local chapters. Our website (www.americanpilgrims. org) is packed with Camino-related information, and our newsletter, *La Concha*, contains members' stories and photos. Our Facebook group has more than 10,000 members helping each other prepare and follow the Camino.

We issue credentials to pilgrims, many of whom go on to become our members or donors. Their dues and contributions help us make grants to support albergues and for other Camino needs, and to provide training for hospitaleros.

American Pilgrim members join you in spirit on the trail and welcome all of you to join us. Together, we will continue to share our enthusiasm for and appreciation of the Camino experience and to support the Camino so that others, like the readers of *Camino to Santiago*, may cherish it in the future.

www.americanpilgrims.org

Australian Friends of the Camino

On St James Day in 2010 a group of Camino enthusiasts met at St James Church in Adelaide, and from that inaugural meeting the Australian Friends of the Camino was founded a year later.

The mission of the group includes promoting an awareness of the Camino de Santiago to fellow Australians, and assisting, encouraging and supporting those interested in the pilgrimage to the shrine of St James in Santiago de Compostela. To this end the organisation issues Pilgrim Credentials to members, along with a quarterly newsletter, and answers queries from interested persons throughout the country.

The group is based in Adelaide, liaising with the numerous groups meeting throughout the country, and is open to all. Distance is a huge challenge in Australia and so, sadly, it is rare for members in one state to visit groups in another. Meeting times are regularly published on the website and in the newsletters.

PO Box 601, Stirling, South Australia, 5152.
Phone +61 (08) 83708182

www.afotc.org

Camino Society Ireland (CSI)

Camino Society Ireland (CSI) is the successor to The Irish Society of the Friends of St James which was founded in 1992 by returned pilgrims to "give something back" to the Camino and to future pilgrims in gratitude for the fellowship and spiritual renewal they had each experienced on their own Camino. The Society fosters an understanding and appreciation of the Camino's related history, art, architecture and music with particular reference to the Irish connection to the Camino, which is long established; there are even references to it in the Annals of the Four Masters. In 2016 the Society will celebrate a connection established at least 800 years ago between Ireland and Santiago.

The Society issues the Pilgrim Passport and offers an opportunity to all those interested in the Camino to meet and share practical information and experiences through information days, the annual St James's Day Mass, an annual lecture on the Camino, a newsletter, an annual dinner and The Book of Pilgrims to Santiago. The Book of Pilgrims is a homage to the ancient Irish tradition of the illuminated manuscript and to all those who – in the words of a ninth-century Irish calligrapher – strove to "turn darkness into light".

Volunteers from the Society also run the Camino Information Centre at Saint James's Church, James Street, Dublin 8. For information on opening times, please look at the Society's website.

We work as a *meitheal* – an old Irish system of neighbourly cooperation which operates not on the basis of orders or instructions, but between equals, each giving what they can, whenever they can, to the Camino.

The Society is non-political, non-sectarian and non-denominational, encompassing all of Ireland, and it is open to all.

www.caminosociety.ie

The Canadian Company of Pilgrims (CCoP)

The Canadian Company of Pilgrims (CCoP) is a non-denominational, volunteer-run association that supports Canadians planning the pilgrimage to Santiago de Compostela, Spain. We share the Canadian representation with l'Association québécoise des pèlerins et amis du Chemin de Saint-Jacques.

The CCoP provides information and generates awareness and interest in the Camino to Santiago de Compostela through a network of chapters across Canada and via its website and Facebook page. Local chapters provide a forum for the exchange of information about the Camino and also offer practical training and information sessions to the interested and to prospective pilgrims. The Company also issues Credenciales (Pilgrim Credentials/Passports) which are recognised by the pilgrimage authorities in Santiago.

www.santiago.ca

The Confraternity of Saint James

The Confraternity of Saint James, based in London, is a registered UK charity. It was the first English-speaking association of pilgrims.

The Confraternity promotes the pilgrimage to Santiago de Compostela throughout Europe and provides support and services to pilgrims through a wide range of services.

Its Practical Pilgrim Days provide a chance for potential pilgrims to meet more experienced pilgrims and to learn more.

On these days and through the website and publications advice is given on what equipment is needed and how to plan your route.

The organisation also provides a regular bulletin to members, and runs an online bookshop and a library.

In addition, the Confraternity promotes research around the subject of St James and the Camino.

Help is also offered to people who might otherwise be unable to undertake the pilgrimage.

The Confraternity publishes guides to many of the routes to Santiago and also runs two refuges for pilgrims, at Gaucelmo and Miraz. These are staffed by CSJ volunteers.

www.csj.org.uk

The Confraternity of Saint James

The Confraternity of St James South Africa (CSJOFSA)

The CSJ of South Africa is a not-for-profit Public Benefit Organisation which aims to assist prospective pilgrims from South Africa who plan to walk any of the medieval pilgrim routes in Europe known as the Camino de Santiago.

The organisation issues the Pilgrim Record, also known as the Pilgrim Passport or the Credencial.

Our aims

To provide information to prospective South African pilgrims who wish to walk any of the pilgrimage routes (in Spain, France and the other European countries where these routes exist) known as the Camino de Santiago.

To support and assist prospective pilgrims.

To encourage the true spirit of pilgrimage in those walking the Camino.

To maintain a register of South Africans who have walked or cycled any part of the Camino pilgrimage routes.

To network with South Africans in various centres that can provide information and to put them in touch with prospective pilgrims who need assistance.

To organise social gatherings in a regional context on a regular basis.

To develop support materials and documentation as required by the members.

To provide links and references to other websites and reading matter relating to the routes.

To liaise with and support other Camino organisations, wherever they may exist.

www.csjofsa.za.org

In the Beginning – My First Camino
Grant Spangler
United States of America..........12

790 Kilometres to Santiago
Silvia Nilsen
South Africa 14

The Rhythm of the Camino
Basil Fallon
Ireland 16

The Yellow Arrows
Laurie Dennett
A Canadian Living in Spain 18

Keeping Going
Janet Leitch
Australia 20

International Fellowship
Jenny Wood
United Kingdom....................... 22

The Journey is the Destination
Tania Veitch
Canada......................................24

Giving and Receiving
Liz and Dick Crean
England 26

Forgiveness
Rebekah Scott
Spain..28

The Dance
Martha Crites and Jim Limardi
United States of America.........30

Coincidences
Sam Pinkerton
Australia 32

Nothing can be Loved at Speed
Lesley Rankin
Ireland 34

Life Changing
Barry Brooks
United States of America.........36

Gifts
Alan Pearce
Australia 38

Forty Years of Pilgrimage and Service
Marion Marples
United Kingdom.......................40

Pilgrim Angels
Blanche Malankowski-Smith,
Ben Smith and Colleen Smith
United States of America.........44

Scallop Shell
Gerry Riordan
Ireland 46

Companions on the Way
Liz Thackwray
England 48

Community
Mary and Albert Cutts
United Kingdom.......................50

A Journey of Peace and Trust
Andrée Lombard
South Africa 52

Dedication
Daniel Lynch
Ireland 54

Helpful Hallucination
Lydia Gillen
Ireland 56

Together
Susan Spencer and
Michelle Herring
United States of America.........58

Lost and Found
Trevor Hockey
United Kingdom.......................60

Friends Forever
Frank Burns
Scotland....................................62

Camino Providence
Robert Fink
Canada.....................................64

Mary had a Donkey
Pauline and Morrell Rosseau
South Africa 66

Walking with Nature
Michelle Courtney
Australia 68

Young Single Female
Yosmar Martinez
United States of America.........70

Room for Everyone
John Rafferty
From Scotland,
living in Spain 72

The End and the Beginning
Kenneil Mitchell
United States of America.........74